Second Breakfast

Chris P Bacon

BookLeaf Publishing

India | USA | UK

Made with ❤ on the BookLeaf Publishing Platform
www.bookleafpub.in
www.bookleafpub.com

Dedication

To my dearest friends and family, thank you for your love and support. To those who inspired these works, I appreciate our experiences together - regardless of the nature of those experiences. I wouldn't be who I am today without you.

Preface

This poetry book is a collection of twenty-one poems written at different points in my life about various non-breakfast topics. These are a variety of personal thoughts; kindly forgive the rawness of the works. The pieces were inspired by tough situations in my life but others from lovely experiences - even if they may not have felt that way at the time. Upon reflection, I suppose the theme of my works is largely centered on loss in different forms (i.e loss of a lover, missed opportunities, failing relationships). which I used poetry to express in abstract in my private journals. As I said, they are raw and largely unedited. Few of my writings were shared with anyone and were left in their original formatting. Because these are basically my inner thoughts, the process of preparing this book was a unique experience for me, especially given the specific nature of subject matter included - notably my complex relationship with my dad. To that and to him, I'll say this, "no hard feelings."

Acknowledgements

I want to thank Zack, Kyle, Liebe, Frank and Victor for being there for me in difficult times. Kyle, thank you for letting me spam you with drafts, and you too Taylor (both Taylors actually) for those after work pep talks. Ipinder, you impromptu therapy sessions were much appreciated. SoCal Taylor, Herr Liebe, and Mr. Fat Fingas Cody, thank you for sticking round, it was an honor and privilege to serve with you. Finally, thank you dear reader for taking the time to read this.

1. The Son's Prayer

Our Father's faith, though deep and strong,
We walk within its hallowed song.
But I have sought another way,
And found a truth that lights my day.

Though you may scorn, and you may cry,
I choose the path where I shall fly.
The chains you gave, I lay them down,
And wear instead a new-found crown.

I seek not guilt, nor fear, nor shame,
But peace that calls me by its name.
In faith I stand, and in it thrive,
For this is where my soul's alive.

Forgive me not for what I've done,
For I have found the truth begun.
I've left behind what once I knew,
To walk in light, to start anew.

I honor you, but I must go,
To seek the winds where new seeds grow.
In freedom's name, my heart will sing,
And find the peace that faith can bring.

Amen

2. Beneath The Cracks

I loved you once, in quiet ways,
Your hands, your voice, your steady gaze.
But then you built a wall too tall,
And left me searching for the fall.

You taught me strength, but it was sharp,
A lesson carved into the dark.
The love you gave, it often stung,
Like bitter words, or songs unsung.

I hated you, or so it seemed,
For every time you crushed my dream,
For every silence, cold and long,
I fought to prove where I belong.

Yet still, within the deepest cracks,
A piece of me comes rushing back.
Your blood runs through my fragile veins,
And in your eyes, I know my pains.

A twisted dance of love and hate,
Our hearts entangled, bound by fate.
I don't forgive, but I don't leave,
Despite all the scars, I still believe.

The mirror cracks, but still reflects,
The love I fought to resurrect.
For even when the rage has passed,
I find I'm yours, and always will be, at last.

3. Serenity

Serenity, with eyes like dusk's soft glow,
A fleeting presence, yet my heart did know
That in your gaze, a quiet grace resides,
A peaceful calm that the world cannot disguise.

You entered like a breeze, so light, so rare,
With soft words that danced like perfume in the air.
In those few moments, time seemed to stand still,
A gentle silence, with beauty to fill.

Though our words were brief, your spirit shone,
A warmth, a light, a place I'd call home.
Serenity, in you the stars align,
A fleeting encounter, yet forever divine.

4. When The Dust Settles

Last night, the music spun its spell,
In notes and rhythms, hearts would swell.
A crowd alive, a sea of sound,
But in the midst, one soul I found.

Pixie, with her gilded hair,
A wisdom wrapped in cool night air.
Her laughter echoed through the beat,
A spark of joy, so bittersweet.

We swayed together, lost in time,
To mysterious strange, haunting rhymes.
Her stories whispered, soft and bright,
As melodies danced through the night.

Her eyes were windows, wide and clear,
To places I had never seen,
A life well-lived, with edges smooth,
Like worn-out pages, yet still new.

And when the concert's pulse did fade,
We walked through quiet streets, afraid
To let the magic slip away,
To lose the spark of yesterday.

But Pixie smiled, and in her gaze,
I saw a world beyond the haze—
Of music, passion, and fleeting friends,
A night where time and truth transcend.

In the crowd, she moved with ease,
A steady grace, a quiet tease,
The music swirled, the bass, the beat,
And in her eyes, I found a heat.

She led me through the crowded floor,
Her laughter rich, her spirit more,
An older soul, so wild and free,
A force that pulled the younger me.

The night unfolded in her hands,
A rhythm only she could command,
We danced, we soared, we lost our place,
The world outside erased by grace.

But dawn arrives, and with it, doubt,
The music fades, the lights burn out,
She slipped away, a whispered breeze,
Leaving only questions, silent pleas.

I searched for her, but she's not there,

Just memories tangled in the air,
Her touch, her smile, her knowing eyes,
A fleeting gift beneath the skies.

What did she want? What did she see?
In me, a spark, or just a plea?
Am I to blame for what was lost,
Or were we both paying the cost?

The ache lingers, but I'm alone,
Dancing still, but on my own,
An older heart, a younger touch,
A bond so brief, yet felt so much.

5. The Silence Between Us

I thought I knew love—
Thought I had it all right,
Built walls around us,
Made sure we'd never fight.

But somewhere, in silence,
I missed what you needed,
Took for granted the soft words
That left you unseated.

I never meant to wound you,
Never meant to cause pain,
But the words I left unsaid
Fell like a storm brewing pouring rain.

You were the one,
The one I could see,
In every dream,
In every breath I breathe.

But now, in the quiet,
I hear the soft sighs,
The distance between us,
The unshed goodbyes.

I never knew how fragile
The heart could really be,
How the smallest of actions
Could bring you to flee.

And now I regret
Every time I was blind,
Every moment I failed
To give you my time.

You were the one—
I should have seen it clear,
But now I'm left waiting,
Wishing you were still near.

If I could go back,
I'd rewrite every word,
But the damage is done,
And silence is heard.

6. The Last Ride

I was born with a six-shooter and a hard day's work,
Raised on the law of the land—rough, no perks.
My father told me, "Son, you ride fast and you fight,
You keep your word and your gun hand tight."

The desert wind whispered of a man's silent pride,
Of toughness in silence, of heart locked inside.
No room for weakness, no time for doubt,
A man's only as good as his courage and clout.

But now, on the edge of this changing new day,
Folks speak of feelings, of words left unsaid,
They say a man's strength ain't measured by steel,
But by what's in his heart, and the wounds that can heal.

I watch from the porch as they build up the town,
New laws, new rules, where no fight can go down.
They talk about peace, but I've lived with the gun,
And peace don't feel like the work I've done.

Am I wrong to stand still, as the world races past?
Should I trade in my pistols, and bury my past?
Or is there a place where a man's still a man,
Not a ghost of the cowboy, but something less planned?

The sunset's the same as it always has been,
But I don't know the land I once called my kin.
The badge of the past, heavy on my chest,
A cowboy just trying to make sense of the rest.

7. Homecoming

I learned to stand firm,
Through fire and fight,
Where men don't cry,
And wrong is made right.

The world was clear then—
Black and white,
Victory or death,
No room for doubt or fright.

But now, I walk these streets,
Where silence is loud,
And the smiles I once trusted
Are veiled in the crowd.

They speak of peace,
Of healing and change,
Of men who speak softly,
And hearts that aren't strange.

I don't know how to wear
This new world's face,
Where gentleness rises
And strength's a slow pace.

In battle, I knew
How to fight and to stand,
But here, in the quiet,
I don't understand.

Where do I place
This weight on my chest?
The uniform I wore,
And the man I thought best?

I fought for a cause,
I bled for the flag,
Now they say I must talk
When I used to just act.

Is my honor lost
In a world that has changed?
Or is there a way
To keep what I've gained?

I carry my scars—
They're part of my soul,
But now I wonder
What makes a man whole

8. The Mourning After

Under neon lights, we moved as one,
The music pulsing, hearts undone,
You laughed, you twirled, you caught my eye,
And for a moment, time slipped by.

The rhythm bound us, skin on skin,
A dance of joy, a fleeting spin,
The world outside no longer there,
Just you, just me, just air, just flare.

But morning comes, and with it, cold,
The memory of a night too bold,
You're gone, a phantom in the light,
And I'm left wondering, was it right?

The dance, it lingers in my chest,
A beat I cannot seem to rest,
Was it a bond, or just a game?
Am I to blame for what became?

Your laughter echoes, then is lost,
The cost of pleasure, the lines we crossed,
What was shared in that fleeting grace?
Now feels like emptiness I chase.

Abandoned, in the silence deep,
I find no answers when I weep,
Just the memory of a song,
Where something real felt all along.

9. Restraint

I stand before you, words unspoken,
A storm inside, yet still unbroken.
My lips are sealed, my heart is tight,
Afraid to shatter this fragile night.

The things I want to say to you,
Are buried deep, but they are true—
The hurt, the shame, the silent screams,
The shattered pieces of my dreams.

If I speak, will you retreat?
Will your love turn cold, incomplete?
Will your anger rise and blind your eyes,
Or will you hear the truth inside?

I fear the weight of every word,
The sound of pain you've never heard.
What if my voice breaks your disguise,
And all our truths we cannot hide?

I want to ask, to beg, to plead,
For understanding, for your need
To see the child beneath the mask,
To answer questions I dare not ask.

But what if what I say will burn,
And leave me lost, with no return?
What if your words, sharp as knives,
Cut the last thread that still survives?

So here I stand, with heart in hand,
Unspoken truths I can't command.
Afraid to speak, afraid to be—
For fear of losing you—and me.

10. Fever Dream

In the quiet after passion fades,
A storm brews deep where warmth once laid,
Her touch, once gentle, now feels like chains,
A tenderness twisted, causing pains.

I wake, confused, in the aftermath,
Wondering where I've gone off path,
Her absence leaves a hollow space,
As if I never knew her face.

A night of fire, of whispered cries,
Now shadows in my aching eyes,
Did she see me, or just the skin?
Was it love, or something thin?

The silence mocks my trembling soul,
A heart once open, now a hole,
I search for answers, but they're gone,
Just echoes of the night that's long.

Abandoned in a world so cold,
The wounds are silent, never told.
And yet, I wonder, can I heal,
When all I feel is lost and real?

The pain, the shame, the question clear—
Did she care, or just disappear?
Each thought a thread I cannot weave,
Caught between what's real and what I believe

11. Unspoken

Beneath the weight of words unkind,
I learned to lock my heart, confined.
A hollow smile, a quiet plea,
To hide the storm inside of me.

They spoke in tones so sharp, so cold,
A truth so bitter, harsh, and bold,
And yet I learned to bow, to bend,
To silence pain, to never send.

Emotions buried deep inside,
A silent ache I cannot hide.
The words they left, they cut and burned,
But I was taught to wait, to turn.

The mirror shows a face so calm,
But in my chest, there's no real balm—
A heart that's cracked, a soul that's bruised,
Yet still, the mask cannot be moved.

The battles fought with no release,
A quiet war, no sign of peace.
I swallow screams, I stifle tears,
And hide my truth in hidden tears.

For they, the ones who ought to see,
Demand that I become the "we"
Of silent hurt and muted cries,
While in my soul, the darkness lies.

But in the quiet, I still fight—
In shadows, I'll reclaim my light.

12. The Price of Loyalty

I stood by you, through days and nights,
With steadfast love, through wrong and right.
I turned away from others' gaze,
To walk beside you through the haze.

I missed the glances, the quiet smiles,
The moments lost in distant miles.
For every love that might have bloomed,
I stayed with you, my heart consumed.

I thought it noble, thought it pure,
This loyalty that would endure.
Yet in my chest, a hollow ache,
As life slipped by for loyalty's sake.

I held the line, but now I see,
What held me close, it held me free.
I shut the doors to love's sweet call,
While you behind them let me fall.

And now the truth, a bitter wind,
The love I trusted had thinned.
You betrayed the vows we made,
And I was left in shadows, played.

For every chance I let slip past,
For every love that couldn't last,
I see your smile, a false disguise—
The lies that danced behind your eyes.

The price of loyalty, so high,
Now haunts me as I wonder why
I gave you all, while you did steal
The pieces of my heart, surreal.

Regret, it cuts with sharper blade,
For all the chances I delayed.
And now the hurt is all I know,
For trusting love where lies could grow.

13. A Father's Shadow, A Mother's Echo

He stands so tall, his words like stone,
A constant roar, a trembling tone.
With every step, he shapes the air,
Yet never sees the weight I bear.

He tells me how, what's wrong, what's right,
Unseen, I fade into the night.
His love a force, too sharp, too bright,
Blinds me to my own quiet fight.

He means no harm, I know it well,
But every word feels like a spell,
I shrink beneath his steady hand,
Lost in a world I never planned.

I long for space, a place to grow,
But he insists, and does not know,
That in his grip, I start to break,
A heart so full, yet hard to wake.

His pride, a shield I cannot pierce,
My voice too small, my thoughts unclear.
Does he not see, does he not hear,

The quiet pain I hold so near?

I turn to her, my softer light,
Hoping her touch will ease the fight.
Her voice, a balm I've longed to hear,
Yet still, I find the shadows near.

She listens close, but does she know
The weight of all I feel below?
Her words are soft, but much the same,
A quiet echo of his name.

She speaks of dreams, of paths to take,
But I am lost, unsure, opaque.
Her love wraps tight, but cannot see
That all I want is space to be.

Her caring wraps me in its warmth,
Yet feels like chains, though soft, still strong.
She whispers hope, but deep inside,
I wonder if it's hers or mine.

In her embrace, I seek relief,
But find the same, unspoken grief.
For all the love, it still remains:
A gentle force that breaks in chains.

I wanted just a place to stand,
Not molded by another's hand.
Yet in her eyes, I see the same—
The silent love, the quiet claim.

14. Before The End

I thought I'd never let you go,
Your laugh, your touch, your steady glow.
But in my heart, a shadow grew,
A longing I could not undo.

You were my light, my endless sky,
Yet still, I asked myself, "Why try?"
For love, at times, felt like a weight,
A burden more than shared fate.

I wanted space, to break away,
To find a self, to breathe, to stray.
But shame would flood me, keep me near,
For fear you'd suffer if I veered.

Then came the day I had to leave—
To cut the ties, to take my reprieve.
You begged me stay, but I was torn,
Not knowing that you'd soon be gone.

Now I stand alone, lost in tears,
Wishing I could undo those years.
The guilt wraps tight, a choking chain,
For in your absence, comes the pain.

Could I have stayed, should I have fought,
For the love I once so fiercely sought?
Now you are gone, and I remain,
With grief that pulses through my veins.

I loved you, yet I let you slip,
Away, like water from my grip.
And now your silence haunts my soul,
A love once full, now paying toll.

For wanting space, for wanting rest,
I failed you, love, and now I'm less.
The guilt of leaving, deep and wide,
Is all I feel, now that you've died.

15. Unshackled

The father's words, a thundered plea,
"Stay here with us, stay true to me.
This faith is all you need, my son,
The path is set, the race is won."

But in the son's heart, the seed had grown—
A truth that he could call his own.
Not born of fear, nor guilt's embrace,
But freedom found in a different place.

He wandered far, beyond the fold,
Where stories whispered, ancient, bold.
A faith that spoke not of control,
But of a heart that could be whole.

"No shame in seeking something new,"
He said aloud, "for this is true.
I've found a peace that feels like light,
A way that fills my soul with might."

The father's eyes, cold with dismay,
"Why turn your back? Why walk away?"
But the son stood firm, no tear to show,
For in his heart, his spirit knew.

"I walk this path, not out of spite,
But because my soul has found its light.
You taught me love, but love is free,
And this new faith sets all of me."

No guilt, no fear, no bond to break,
For in this choice, his heart does wake.
The chains were never his to wear—
In truth, he breathes a different air.

The father rages, still, and cries,
But the son no longer needs disguise.
For he has chosen, with open eyes,
To walk a road where he can rise.

No guilt, no shame, no chains to bear—
The son stands free, with heart laid bare.

16. The Command

The father prays, his voice a storm,
A sacred rite to keep him warm.
"Stay in the fold," he sternly pleads,
"Follow the path of ancient deeds."

But in the son's heart, a quiet spark,
A longing born within the dark.
He hears a call from distant shores,
A faith unknown, with open doors.

The father's eyes, like burning coals,
See not the struggle in his soul.
"To stray from this," he warns with care,
"Is to lose your way, to forfeit prayer."

Yet whispers rise, soft as a breeze,
In foreign temples, among the trees.
The son, torn in faith's tight grasp,
Desires to let go, to unclasp.

A new horizon calls his name,
A different truth, a different flame.
But fear wraps tight around his chest,
For what he seeks may not be blessed.

He dreams of peace, a different way,
Of opening his heart to pray,
But every step feels like a sin,
For what if he is wrong within?

The father's voice, a thundered sound,
"Stay true, stay safe, stay on this ground."
Yet the son knows, with trembling heart,
That seeking truth is no betrayal, no part.

In silence, he makes a secret vow,
To search for faith, to find it now.
But guilt will cling, and love will burn,
For a son who must wait his turn.

Still, deep inside, he knows the cost—
The faith of one may be the faith of loss.

17. Freedom's Cry

With open scripture, he speaks with force,
Each word a whip, a guiding course.
"Walk this path," he says, "and do not stray,
For God demands it, night and day."

The son, though young, feels heavy chains,
Woven from faith, but laced with pains.
Each prayer a prison, each rule a wall,
A God of love, but one who calls

Not to embrace, but to obey,
To bow his head, to kneel and pray.
The father's voice, a steadfast guide,
Yet in its echo, truth is tied.

The son asks why, but fear holds tight,
The answer buried deep in night.
"Because I say, and God is right,"
The father's rule, the final light.

Yet in his heart, the son does ache,
For freedom's voice, for love's own sake.
But trapped beneath his father's creed,
He wonders, does faith bind or feed?

A silent cry, a muted plea,
"Is faith my choice, or destiny?"
For in the father's grasp so tight,
The son must learn to see the light

18. Woven In Fire

A love so fierce, yet hard to bear,
A father's gaze, so cold, so rare.
His hands, though firm, would shape my soul,
In ways I never could control.

He speaks in tones that cut like knives,
His silence louder than my cries.
A life of rules, no room to stray,
Yet still, I chase his distant way.

His love a storm, both wild and deep,
In whispered moments, ours to keep.
Yet shadows linger, words unspoken,
A bond unbroken, though unspoken.

I long for warmth, a gentle touch,
But he, like stone, remains too much.
A love entwined with bitter strife,
He molds me still, this father's life.

But in his eyes, I see the fight,
The distant glow of faded light.
And though I rage, and though I burn,
I crave his love, and yet I yearn.

For love and hate are woven tight,
A father's heart, both wrong and right.

19. Fading Into You

You speak in riddles, words that twist,
A world that drifts, a fogged-up mist.
I reach for you, but you're not there,
Your eyes are distant, lost in air.

Once, you were whole, just like me,
Laughter and games, wild and free.
Now you're a shadow in the night,
Chasing whispers, fleeing light.

I watch you fight, but can't explain
The battles you wage inside your brain.
You say they're watching, you say they're near,
I try to comfort, but I too fear.

In the silence, I feel you fade,
Like a dream that time has made.
I wish I could take the weight you bear,
But I can't enter that fragile air.

I want to help, to pull you back,
But your reality's out of track.
I hold your hand, though you don't see,
I'll stand beside you—always, silently.

You are my brother, lost and found,
In this strange world that spins around.
Though your mind may wander far away,
In my heart, you'll always stay.

Through the quiet storm, we walk as two,
One lost, one searching—me and you.
No cure for this, no easy way,
But I'll love you more with each passing day.

20. Half Mast

Twelve funerals, each a quiet toll,
A whispered grief, a heavy soul.
The air is thick with unsaid prayers,
And memories linger, unaware.

Twelve souls, now distant, out of sight,
Each one a star, now lost to night.
A dozen times, the earth did sigh,
As we said goodbye, and wondered why.

The flowers faded, tears were shed,
Each heart broken, but not yet dead.
Through silent streets, the mourners tread,
Their footsteps echoing the things unsaid.

Twelve funerals, a slow refrain,
Of love and loss, of joy and pain.
Yet still, we live, we carry on,
With twelve names fading at the dawn.

21. Celestial Grace

Her sublime beauty extends beyond race or color
A mysterious smile to enthrall
Like the calmness of an undiscovered ocean;
Sea of dreams,
Azure mercury flowing quick over grainy sands
Gently caressing the ivory shore
Leaving seductive ink blots dotting the surface

Eyes that shine like two stars
Above against a velvet sky -
Although distant like pearls
On the neck of a goddess,
Rare and priceless masterpieces

A hypnotic sight meant to be cherished
With unadulterated bliss pervading
In every fiber of one's being
Illuminating radiant grace
That makes one abandon their nothingness
To see the world crawl to a standstill,
Their life becoming an afterthought

Callously collapsing,
Moment by moment,

In every glance -
A chapter in time,
In every blink -
Poetry in motion,

Left wondering how nature's perfect bloom,
A plum rose kissed by an angel
Sent from The Most High,
Invaded their sanctum of solace.